Life Cycle of a

Sunflower

Angela Royston

Heinemann
LIBRARY

First published in Great Britain by Heinemann Library
Halley Court, Jordan Hill, Oxford OX2 8EJ,
a division of Reed Educational and Professional Publishing Ltd.

Heinemann is a registered trademark of Reed Educational and Professional
Publishing Limited.

Oxford   Melbourne   Auckland   Kuala Lumpur   Singapore
Ibadan   Nairobi   Kampala   Johannesburg   Gaborone
Portsmouth NH (USA)   Chicago

Designed by Celia Floyd
Illustrations by Alan Fraser
Printed in Hong Kong / China

02
10 9 8 7 6 5 4

ISBN 0 431 08368 1

British Library Cataloguing in Publication Data

Royston, Angela
Life cycle of a sunflower
1. Sunflowers – Juvenile literature
I. Title II. Sunflower
583.9'9

Acknowledgements
The Publisher would like to thank the following for permission to reproduce
photographs:
A–Z Botanical Collection Ltd/Joyce Hammond pg 14; Bruce Coleman Ltd/S Nielsen
pg 11; FLPA/Gerard Lacz pg 18; Harry Smith Collection pg 20; Holt Studios
International/Nigel Cattlin pgs 5, 7, 8, 10, 15, 19, 21, 26-27; NHPA/A N T pg 16,
NHPA/Roger Tidman pg 23, NHPA/Christophe Ratier pg 24, NHPA/K Ghani pg 25;
Oxford Scientific/Stephen Downer pgs 9, 12, 13, Oxford Scientific/Martyn Chillmaid
pg 17, Oxford Scientific/Patti Murray pg 22; Roger Scruton pg 6; The Garden Picture
Library/Chris Burrows pg 4.

Cover photograph: Tony Stone Images/Karen Smith.

Our thanks to Dr John Feltwell, Wildlife Matters Consultancy, for his comments in
the preparation of this edition.

Contents

What is a sunflower?

Sunflowers are tall plants with
large, flat flowers. They come from
North America but now grow in
other parts of the world too.

There are several kinds of
sunflowers, but the sunflower in this
book has bright yellow petals. All
sunflowers grow from large seeds.

8 weeks

10 weeks

13 weeks

Spring

The seed is planted in the ground in spring, when the soil is warm and damp. Inside the seed is a tiny plant which soon begins to grow.

3 days

1 week

6 weeks

The **roots** of the plant push down through the soil. They are covered in tiny hairs which take in water. A green shoot grows upwards.

8 weeks

10 weeks

13 weeks

1–2 weeks

The green shoot has pushed through the soil. The first leaves open out. They use sunlight, air and water to make food for the plant.

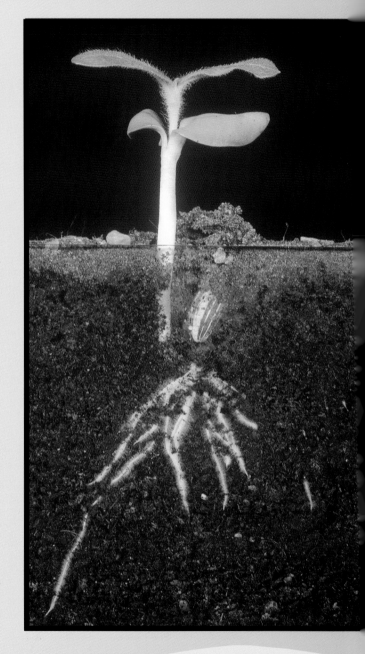

3 days

1 week

6 weeks

The plant grows taller and more leaves grow at the tip of the stem. The stem is covered with fine hairs to stop insects from climbing up it.

8 weeks

10 weeks

13 weeks

4–6 weeks

The leaves grow bigger. Under the ground, the **roots** grow longer. They take in the water and **minerals** the plant needs to stay alive and go on growing.

3 days

I week

6 weeks

A large bud has formed at the end of the stem. It is protected by pointed green **bracts** that look like small leaves.

8 weeks

10 weeks

13 weeks

6–8 weeks

The **bracts** unfold and the bud begins to open.

3 days

I week

6 weeks

Underneath the bracts are lots of yellow petals.

8 weeks

10 weeks

13 weeks

9 weeks

The plant grows taller and taller. The flowers open out. Each **flower-head** contains many tiny flowers.

14

3 days

1 week

6 weeks

All the sunflowers turn to face
the sun. As the sun moves across
the sky, the flower-heads turn to
follow it.

8 weeks

10 weeks

13 weeks

Summer

Each **flower-head** is made up of hundreds of tiny flowers called **florets**. The tips of these florets are covered with a fine yellow dust called **pollen**.

3 days

I week

6 weeks

The flower-head is growing bigger. Honey bees see the bright yellow petals and come to the flower-head to collect pollen.

8 weeks

10 weeks

13 weeks

10 weeks

As the honey bee crawls across the **florets**, its body and legs become covered with **pollen**. The bee flies from one **flower-head** to another.

3 days

1 week

6 weeks

The pollen rubs off its body into the florets. In the centre of each floret is a tiny **ovule**. The ovule becomes a seed when the **pollen** joins with it.

8 weeks

10 weeks

13 weeks

13 weeks

The **florets** have no **pollen** left, but inside each one a seed is beginning to swell. The petals round the **flower-head** wilt and fall off.

3 days

1 week

6 weeks

The flower-heads become darker and turn almost black. Some of them are so heavy they droop from the end of the stems.

8 weeks

10 weeks

13 weeks

14 weeks

The **florets** wither too. The **flower-head** is now a flat disk of shiny black seeds.

3 days

1 week

6 weeks

Birds feed on the seeds. The birds drop some of the seeds as they fly away. These may grow into new plants next year.

8 weeks

10 weeks

13 weeks

16 weeks

The farmer has come to **harvest** the sunflower seeds. The harvester cuts the plants and shakes out the seeds.

3 days

1 week

6 weeks

The harvester missed this plant!
The leaves wither and die. Some of
the seeds that fall to the ground will
grow into new plants next spring.

8 weeks   10 weeks   13 weeks

A field of sunflowers

Farmers grow sunflowers for their seeds. Most of the seeds are crushed and made into animal feed or squeezed to make sunflower oil.

Some seeds are roasted for us to eat as snacks. Pet guinea pigs like to eat sunflower seeds too. Some seeds are kept to be planted next spring.

Life cycle

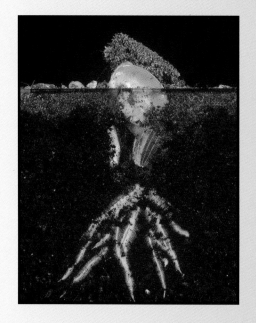

3 days

1 week

6 weeks

8 weeks **10 weeks**

13 weeks

Fact file

Sunflowers can grow over 7 metres tall – taller than a one-storey house.

The **flower-head** can be 30 to 40 centimetres across – as big as a dinner plate.

Each flower-head may produce 1,000 seeds. Most seeds are made into oil and margarine.

Sunflowers grow all over the world but more are grown in Russia than in any other country.

Glossary

bracts parts of a plant that protect the bud while it grows. In most other kinds of flowers they are called sepals

floret a tiny flower, which is part of a **flower-head**

flower-head a flower that is made up of many tiny **florets**

harvest to gather in ripe crops

minerals chemicals that the plant needs to stay healthy

ovule female egg that forms a seed when joined with a male pollen

pollen the tiny male seeds of a plant

roots the parts of a plant that grow under the ground and take in water

Index